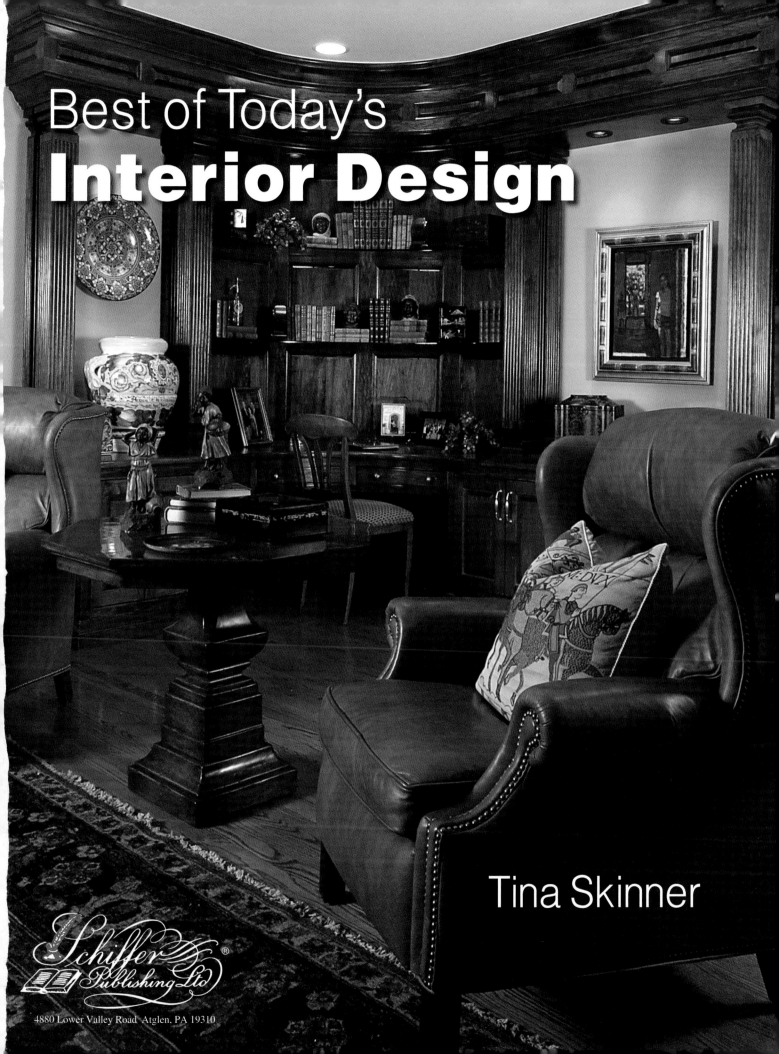

Best of Today's
Interior Design

Tina Skinner

Schiffer Publishing Ltd

4880 Lower Valley Road Atglen, PA 19310

Other Schiffer Books by Tina Skinner

Beautiful Bathrooms. ISBN: 0764315366. $24.95

Beautiful Bedrooms: Design Inspirations from the World's Leading Inns and Hotels. ISBN: 0764314610. $29.95

Big Book of Kitchen Design Ideas. ISBN: 0764306723. $24.95

Fire Spaces: Design Inspirations for Fireplaces and Stoves. ISBN: 076431694X. $34.95

Great Kitchen Designs: A Visual Feast of Ideas and Resources. ISBN: 0764312111. $29.95

Home Office, Library, and Den Design. ISBN: 076431842X. $24.95

Kids' Decor: Interior Inspirations, Infants through Teens. ISBN: 0764316133. $24.95

Showhouse Review: An Exposé of Interior Decorating Events. ISBN: 9780764328640. $44.95

Other Schiffer Books on Related Subjects

Designer Showcase: Interior Design at its Best. Melissa Cardona and Nathaniel Wolfgang-Price. ISBN: 0764323989. $44.95

Inside Art Deco: A Pictorial Tour of Deco Interiors from their Origins to Today. Lucy D. Rosenfeld. ISBN: 0764322753. $49.95

Inspired High-End Interior Design. Shane Reilly. ISBN: 0764324993. $44.95

Inspiring Interiors 1950s: From Armstrong. C. Eugene Moore. ISBN: 0764304585. $29.95

Copyright © 2009 by Schiffer Publishing
Library of Congress Control Number: 2008939584

Designed by John P. Cheek
Cover design by Bruce Waters
Type set in Bernhard Modern BT/Humanist 521 BT

ISBN: 978-0-7643-3189-3
Printed in China

Schiffer Books are available at special discounts for bulk purchases for sales promotions or premiums. Special editions, including personalized covers, corporate imprints, and excerpts can be created in large quantities for special needs. For more information contact the publisher:

Published by Schiffer Publishing Ltd.
4880 Lower Valley Road
Atglen, PA 19310
Phone: (610) 593-1777; Fax: (610) 593-2002
E-mail: Info@schifferbooks.com

For the largest selection of fine reference books on this and related subjects, please visit our web site at **www.schifferbooks.com**
We are always looking for people to write books on new and related subjects. If you have an idea for a book please contact us at the above address.

This book may be purchased from the publisher.
Include $5.00 for shipping.
Please try your bookstore first.
You may write for a free catalog.

In Europe, Schiffer books are distributed by
Bushwood Books
6 Marksbury Ave.
Kew Gardens
Surrey TW9 4JF England
Phone: 44 (0) 20 8392-8585; Fax: 44 (0) 20 8392-9876
E-mail: info@bushwoodbooks.co.uk
Website: www.bushwoodbooks.co.uk
Free postage in the U.K., Europe; air mail at cost.

Contents

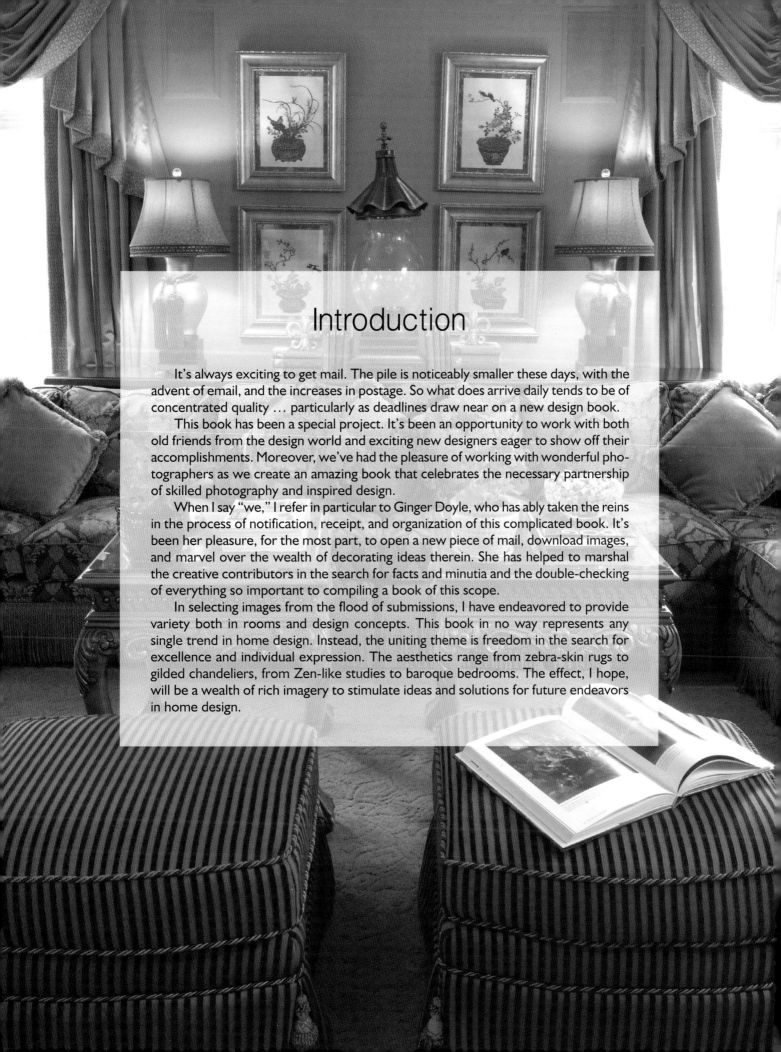

Introduction

It's always exciting to get mail. The pile is noticeably smaller these days, with the advent of email, and the increases in postage. So what does arrive daily tends to be of concentrated quality … particularly as deadlines draw near on a new design book.

This book has been a special project. It's been an opportunity to work with both old friends from the design world and exciting new designers eager to show off their accomplishments. Moreover, we've had the pleasure of working with wonderful photographers as we create an amazing book that celebrates the necessary partnership of skilled photography and inspired design.

When I say "we," I refer in particular to Ginger Doyle, who has ably taken the reins in the process of notification, receipt, and organization of this complicated book. It's been her pleasure, for the most part, to open a new piece of mail, download images, and marvel over the wealth of decorating ideas therein. She has helped to marshal the creative contributors in the search for facts and minutia and the double-checking of everything so important to compiling a book of this scope.

In selecting images from the flood of submissions, I have endeavored to provide variety both in rooms and design concepts. This book in no way represents any single trend in home design. Instead, the uniting theme is freedom in the search for excellence and individual expression. The aesthetics range from zebra-skin rugs to gilded chandeliers, from Zen-like studies to baroque bedrooms. The effect, I hope, will be a wealth of rich imagery to stimulate ideas and solutions for future endeavors in home design.

Kitchens

Cucina Italiano

A kitchen's decor harkens to France's rural Province region, with a grand display of the region's colorful pottery, and a wine rack stocked with one of its finest products. The kitchen and dining room combination was handsomely outfitted with lots of storage space, with cabinets spanning each wall, and a central island console with built-in cupboards. Beneath the stove's wood-encased hood, a tile mosaic adds traditional beauty, while the antiqued finish of the island lends a rustic appearance to its fluted pilasters. Above, a wrought-iron fixture sheds light on the countertop.

Design: Eleanore Berman, ASID, Design 2 Interiors
Photography: Russell Abraham

Captivating Cuisine

The highlights of this gorgeous kitchen are in the fine cabinetry that covers each wall: elegantly carved details on the custom island, a beautiful mantle above the range, and rich crown moulding ringing all. The island has been designed to give the appearance of a piece of furniture, and has two levels of granite countertop to facilitate food preparation by multiple chefs. Stainless steel appliances are a clean, modern accent in this classic space, and are integrated seamlessly into the overall look. Carved wooden columns, for example, flank the stove. On the marble tile floor, a throw rug matches the tan and amber tones of the flecked granite counters.

Design: Gwen Nagorsky, ASID of Directions in Design, Inc.
Photography: Peter Rymwid

Island Re-Treat

A palatial kitchen circles round a central island created in fine furniture fashion. Upholstered chairs gather round a sunlit breakfast nook nearby.

Design: Agostino's Design Group
Photography: Randall Perry

Tonal Cuisine

Three colors interplay in this kitchen, creating a dramatic visual theme. Roosters in a ceiling border and a plant are among the touches that add hominess to the setting, but the strict discipline of maintaining a color scheme helps keep this room, traditionally a clutter magnet, clear.

Design: Pricilla Fried Interior Design/Staging
Photography: Ivy D Photography, Inc.

French Country Kitchen

The mood is light in this charming kitchen, with whimsical details that caricaturize its rural French style. Wine aficionados, the owners decided on a cask theme when they put a wood façade over their refrigerator, complete with the carved inscription *In Vino Veritas* (In wine there is truth). Another amusing element is the island, designed to resemble a market cart, with its dual wheels and rustic paintjob. In one corner, a sewer grate from Paris has been incorporated in the tiled floor as a curiosity, and serves as a conversation piece when entertaining guests. The hood over the stainless steel range takes the appearance of a miniature building, and houses a spice rack on the inside.

Design: Scott Cohen, Green Scene Landscape

The Right Circles

Small on space, this kitchen is big on performance, and with a sense of style and humor to boot. A central island is a standout, with its red stain finish and its incredible slice-of-pie workstation ethic, from the central sink to the raised cutting board. Storage underneath comes in handy, too. Water is at the ready both in the center of the room and on the wall above the professional cook top, ready to top off big pots of pasta, or simmering risotto creations.

Design: Judith Designs, Ltd.
Photography: Ivy D Photography, Inc.

Open Air Theater

A big open kitchen creates a sense of almost being outdoors. Windows help, as does a high ceiling and a complete absence of wall cabinetry. The only wall adornment, in fact, is a mosaic of nature-toned tiles, while a granite countertop on the huge central island imitates the sandy tones found in nature. A rustic dining table and simplistic, Asian-style bar stools emphasize the natural beauty that inspired this kitchen hangout.

Design: Katharine Posillico McGowan, Katharine Jessica Interior Design, LLC
Photography: Ivy D Photography, Inc.

Tuscan Retreat

Family and friends are invited to share in this old-world environment, where faux wall finishes add a patina of antiquity to an assemblage of antiques and hand-painted pottery. Modern in its appliance, the kitchen cabinetry hides all but the massive, professional-level cook center. The refrigerator is concealed behind wood panels, and other amenities are tucked under the marble countertop.

Design: Joyce Hoshall Interiors, ASID
Photography: Dave Adams

Super-size Kitchen

An enormous interconnected space provides a cheerful gathering place for friends and family. A coffered ceiling creates an *al fresco* atmosphere, and gleaming cherry cabinetry adds a warm glow.

Design: Linda Kleeman, ASID, Kleeman &
  Associates Interior Design
Photography: Dave Adams

Petite Patisserie

A small kitchen is viewed inside a green frame from the room beyond. Within, glass fronts in wall cabinetry help to add a sense of space, and a small window admits daylight. Simple shaker-style cabinet doors conceal a wealth of storage space. By locating the sink in a corner, more workspace is preserved on the countertop.

Design: Peg Seropian, Metropolitan Cabinet & Countertop
Contractor: Phil Rothschild of P.D. Builders

New with Age

Dark woodwork feels centuries old, yet this kitchen is as new and modern as any cook could hope for. Behind panels, a double fridge stores fresh and frozen goods, and the arched hearth is home to a professional cook range. Crown moulding and craftsman carved details give this room its rich flavor and sense of history, though its only just now in the making.

Design: Sara Dickinson, Morgan House Interiors
Photography Paul S. Bartholomew

The limited space available for this loft kitchen was put to stylish use, with blonde cabinetry offset by blue accents.

Design by Joani Stewart, ASID, IIDA, Montana Avenue Interiors
Photography: Douglas Hill

Modern Cuisine

A cubist approach to kitchen design adds
texture and symmetry to this gleaming kitchen.
Black and white further enhances the space,
emphasizing the ceiling height and allowing the
cool bar stools to really stand out.

Design: Diane Paparo Associates
Photography: Immagine 3

Country Kitchen

Checkered wallpaper and green accents add a natural charm to this informal kitchen. Its casual-nature serves as a platform to celebrate elegance, however, in a range hood outlined handsomely in wood moulding, an artful window nook flanked by windowed display cabinets, and a central island capped with artfully crafted wood countertop with a complex, and comfortable, edge.

Design: Joan Spiro, ASID Professional Member,
* Joan Spiro Interiors*
Photography: Ivy D Photography, Inc.

Tropical Island

Soft fennel green unites a kitchen/living space
accented by reds and blacks, and underscored
in warm wood tones. Houseplants flourish
along the sunlit outer wall, lending the interior
a sense of tropic lushness.

Design: Peter Amedore, Amedore Homes
Photography: Randall Perry

Back to the Future

Glass and steel add walls of wow to this futuristic kitchen. Red chairs create a human element, and an invitation to enter this incredible culinary center.

Design: Stephan Green, AIA, Clark & Green, Inc.
Photography: Randall Perry

Country Catch

A mix of antiques brings a sense of tradition to a kitchen furnished with fresh white kitchen cabinetry.

Design: Linda Dickerson Interiors, ASID, IDS
Photos by Steven Paul Whitsitt

Check It Out

A kitchen shines with the best-to-be-had elements – a wood and tile parquet floor, granite slab countertop as well as a wood work stations, fine cabinetry, gilded hardware, and a stone and wood structure designed to impress. A wealth of under-counter cabinetry makes it easy to keep all the cookware and staples out of sight.

Design: Jack McKernon, McKernon Design
*   *Associates*
Photography: Randall Perry

Asian aesthetics are married to European in a kitchen focused as much on the view beyond as it is on itself.

Design: Cheryl A. Van Duyne Interior Design
Photography: Danny Piassick

Dining
Rooms

Plush Elegance

The fresco-painted, floral accented ceiling is the dramatic highlight of this elegant dining room, with dual chandeliers that add to the old-world charm of the space. Richly upholstered chairs provide seating around a classic table, the dark crimson velvet offsetting the creamy tiles below. Crown moulding with scalloped accents completes the room, with a finish that complements the beige hues of the ceiling.

Design: Christi Johaningmeyer, Architextures, LLC
Photography: Jeff Green Photography

Everything in this modern dining room has been arranged to show off the magnificent paintings that grace four neutral white walls. Creatively understated lighting shines through a glass table with striking green leather chairs that circle a seashell centerpiece.

Design: Bruce Norman Long
Photography: John Armich

Modern-Day Mead Hall

The oblong shape of this dining room provided its owners with a unique opportunity to infuse the space with character. With a long table capable of seating ten, a gray-brick fireplace that suggests a castle keep, and a pseudo-heraldic wall hanging, the room plays with a light-hearted medieval ambiance, updated with multi-colored hanging lights and a bright area rug. On the table, a blown-glass bowl adds artistic flair, catching the light from a set of French doors.

Design: Roslyn Schineiderman, ASID, NCIDQ, RS Design
Photography: John Armich

Metallic tones create timeless accents in a classic, formal dinner setting.

Design: Peter Amedore, Amedore Homes
Photography: Randall Perry

The potential of a narrow space was maximized with recessed cabinetry and sleek minimalist décor. The dining room/kitchen combination is as attractive as it is functional. A long wooden table seats eight, beneath understated modern light fixtures. Pocket doors separate the dining area from the hallway, contributing to the vaguely Eastern aesthetic. Moreover, the kitchen is accessible over a shared counter surface, making entertaining a snap. When greater separation is desired, a folding screen can be stretched across the counter.

Design: Peter Budeiri and Associates, Architecture
Photography: Jennifer Krogh

Deco Dining Room

Silver and gold accents and an art deco aesthetic sensibility help this dining room hearken back to another era and creates the perfect environment for entertaining. The circular '20s-style mirror, with its extravagant sunburst frame, lights up the room and its elegantly simple antique furnishings. Sconces decked out with hanging crystals flank a massive oil painting. Block glass lights along the ceiling allow natural light to filter into this enormously tall room during the day.

Design: Maureen Console' ASID, M. Console' Interiors
Photography: Ivy D Photography, Inc.

Combination Magic

This attractive dining and living room combination makes the most of its open design, with abundant floor space and big windows to keep the space bright and cheery. Light-colored hardwood floors enhance this sense of openness, and ensure that neither diners nor loungers feel cramped. Spacious arched windows are emphasized with treatments that scallop their enormous outlines. A striking crystal chandelier overhangs the custom round dining room table, surrounded by comfortably upholstered chairs.

Design: Maureen Console', ASID, M. Console'
  Interiors
Photography: Ivy D Photography, Inc.

Old World Opulence

Under a massive crystal chandelier, the dining room table, with its gold accents and intricately carved edge, provides a place to eat amidst rare and historic luxury. The red-painted walls, with their elegantly paneled wainscoting, and an antique Oriental rug ties the color scheme together.

Design: Pricilla Fried Interior Design/Staging
Photography: Ivy D Photography, Inc.

Rich tones in rust, red, and wood create the glow in this room. The warm colors suffuse social gatherings and complement everyone's complexion.

Design: Glenn Lawson, Inc.
Photography: Ivy D Photography, Inc.

Delightful Dining

Quirky and delightful furnishings display an owner's willingness to take risks while sparing nothing in terms of style and craftsmanship. Pretty petals illuminate the stylish wood-grain banquet table, and cubist accents recall Picasso's delightful art.

Design: Judith Designs, Ltd.
Photography: Ivy D Photography, Inc.

Pretty French textiles are warmer than the sunshine streaming through the semicircle of windows in this sweet breakfast nook. While the room bumps out into the garden beyond, the curtains stand ready to preserve a sense of intimacy within.

Design: Kenneth/Davis Architecture and Interior Design
Photography: Peter Chin

Buffet Balance

Charcoal and chocolate hues work in repeating squares in a dining room set to stun. The spacious room offers up artwork from every angle, and an opportunity for friends to relax on comfortable furnishings while enjoying them.

Design: Victor Liberatore, NCIDQ, Professional Member ASID, Victor Liberatore Interior Design
Photography: Alan Gilbert

A mountaintop retreat aura is created by knotty pine paneling and warm earthen tones. For dining, chair backs were sacrificed to secure the view through pretty picture windows.

Design: Stephen Pararo, ASID, IIDA, and Zach Azpeitia, Pineapple House Interior Design
Photography: Scott Moore

Sun Tea

Bright, cheerful yellows imbue this dining area with altruistic motives. White icing in the curtains, chandeliers, and crown moulding perfect this confectionary room.

Design: Kelley Proxmire, Kelley Interior Designs
Photography: Angie Seckinger

An opulent setting provides seating for eight, and plenty of room to extend the table. Red curtains cast their glow over furnishings upholstered in a tapestry-like floral motif.

Design: Agostino's Design Group
Photography: Randall Perry

Close-Knit

Vertical stripes add height to an intimate dining space. Bench seating was upholstered to encourage guests to linger while allowing more friends to elbow in around the table.

Denise by Denise Palumbo, Plum and Crimson Interior Design
Photography: Randall Perry

Taking a cue from the hand-painted splendor of an antique hutch, this room plays with formal wallpapers and oversized country ginghams in an elegant nod to the most popular color.

Design: Debra J. Stein, ASID, Debra J. Interiors
Photography: Randall Perry

Pristine Setting

Warm white textiles add crisp yet comforting
appeal to this formal dining room. The octagonal
shape of the architectural bump out is emphasized
with a domed ceiling highlighted with tonal wood.

Design: Kane Custom Homes
Photography: Randall Perry

Delightful lemon tones enliven a small dining area. Antiqued chairs lend informal enticement to the colorful, fun atmosphere.

Design: Kira Krümm Interior Design
Photography: Randall Perry

Fishing Around

Ultra mod excitement is created with furnishings, while a circular theme seems to stir up the carp in fengshui style.

Design: Kira Krümm Interior Design
Photography: Randall Perry

Eight are democratically seated in this wood-encased dining area.

Design: Maxine Corbett, ASID, IIDA, NCIDQ,
   Richlin Interiors
Photography: Randall Perry

Blondes Have More Fun

Blonde wood and clean lines create a mid-century sensibility for this dining area. Folding doors are space savers, preserving the open feel of the room.

Design: Phillip Smerling Design
Photography: Randall Perry

Gallery Opening

Crimson and gold make a bold statement in this dining room, where art is omni-present, even under the table.

Design: Bill Swietek
Photos by Steven Paul Whitsitt

Golden chrysanthemums gild the chairs amidst a stylish collection of art – the bowl, the lamp, and the chest may function, but they draw awe first.

*Design: Gail Shields Miller, Shields & Company
  Interiors*
Photos by Ben Ritter Photography

Spatially Rich

An expansive dining room tapers up to stacked crown moulding and hand-painted flourishes. A gilded peacock fan delicately shields a massive marble fireplace.

Design: Cheryl A. Van Duyne Interior Design
Photography: Danny Piassick

Timeless Elegance

Art Deco meets the Orient in a room that defies age while gracefully accommodating selected antiques.

Design: Peter Amedore, Amedore Homes
Photography: Randall Perry

Sun drenched foliage and southern splendor meet in a comfortable dining area awash in shades of green.

Design: Lindy Thomas Interiors
Photography: Randall Perry

Iron Supplement

Wrought iron lighting and doors create a solid sense of character for this dining area, while a beam helps define the space.

Design: Leah Bailey, ASID, Pineapple House Interior Design
Photography: Scott Moore

64

Formal
Living
Rooms

A King's Handsome

A hand-knotted rug and an intricately wrought iron chandelier recall castle keeps of centuries ago. Furnishings convey a formal air, while still managing to be comfortable.

Design: Leah Bailey, ASID, Pineapple House Interior Design
Photography: Scott Moore

Jewel tones and a taste of the Orient add to
a room Aladdin would have been proud to
discover.

Design: Teal Michel Interior Design
Photography: Ben Edmonson

Color Chart

A compass rug establishes a color wheel for the
room, echoed in golds, reds, and warm neutrals
on the rise to a pretty picture window.

*Design: Soo Kyung Cho, Metro Asset
    Management, Inc.
Photos by Steven Paul Whitsitt*

Venetian splendor in marbled tones highlight this seaside seating area.

Design: Pamela Crocket Interior Services
Photography: Randall Perry

Silken Splendor

Pleated silk walls cocoon a formal seating area, warmed by a grated fire, and made elegant by faux marble columns and coffered ceiling.

Design: Diane Boyer Interiors, LLC
Photos by Phillip Ennis

Art and Romance

Red-infuses a room with romance amidst a displayed sculptural feline and silk pillows. A chaise lounge acts as a room divider, and provides open invitation to this intimate living area.

Design: Agostino's Design Group
Photography: Randall Perry

Heightened Awareness

Painted beams outline the soaring gambrel ceiling of a great room, while red accents emphasize each pretty gathering in swags that outline the windows. An enormous mirror reflects the wealth of light that hits the wall above a marble hearth.

Design: Peter Amedore, Amedore Homes
Photography: Randall Perry

A chandelier illuminates a formal seating area, enlivened by the natural light from two walls of windows.

Design: Debra J. Stein, ASID, Debra J. Interiors
Photography: Randall Perry

White Feels Right

Modern art and antique mirrors create an impressive juxtaposition of the fireplace focal wall. Window treatments of sheer material allow light to filter through the room and highlight the beautiful white tones of the furniture and rug.

Design: A.J. Margulis, ASID Allied, Deborah Leamann Interiors
Photography: Tom Grimes

Talk about a centerpiece – an antique table with a pretty new blue finish becomes the center of attention in a room furnished for feminine occasions. The perfect place to take tea, carry on book club discussions, or conduct a fireside chat; this lakefront retreat is on everyone's favorite list.

Design: Kenneth/Davis Architecture and Interior Design
Photography: Jeffrey Colquhoun

Fireside Chat

By installing paneled storage units on either side of a fireplace, these homeowners gained a wealth of storage. The antiqued finish on cabinetry and fireplace surround helps minimize their dominance, and allows the large picture window and the great stretch of French doors to add a greater sense of space and openness to this gathering area.

Design: Eva Glaser, Eva & You Interior Design
Photography: Ivy D Photography, Inc.

Modern Masterpiece

This sleek living room, with its panoramic view of the Arizona skyline, proves the old expression that "less is more." Furniture and décor is rigorously sparse and simple, consisting of a few carefully chosen chairs, a leather couch, and a wonderful grand piano. Clean white walls enhance the effect, while a square red area rug adds a fantastic splash of color. In one corner, a telescope on a tripod is poised to observe the wide-open night sky. Amid a wall of glass windows, a door provides easy access to the front porch and patio, where quiet and serenity abound.

Design: Ibarra Rosano Design Architects, Inc.
Photography: Bill Timmerman

Bright Finds

Whites and sun tones team up in a room to
warm any gathering.

Design: Kira Krümm Interior Design
Photography: Randall Perry

This apartment room successfully combines the clean lines of modern design and the comfortable ambiance of home, with abstract artwork hanging from the walls and cozy furniture. The living area, with its sleek glass coffee table, is a gathering place for friends and family, made warmer and more inviting by a calfskin rug and an expansive wall of windows.

Design: Eric J. Schmidt Interiors
Photography: Ivy D Photography, Inc.

Ecclectic Cool

Tri-toned furnishings provide a warm vantage point of a garden room beyond the glass doors. The earthy atmosphere works off Japanned wood tables and chairs, softened by chenille and fur. Exotic dark mouldings, Japanned-black wood finishes, and an ashlar stone fireplace surround create the foundation for a room that is at once exotic and earthy. The comfortable nature of the chairs makes the room inviting while at the same time novel.

Furnishings and Color by Leslie Kalish, LMK Interiors
*   *and Jeanette Ugarte, Leku Eder*
Designed and built by Marilyn Guardunio, CKD, J.B.
*   *Turner & Sons*
Photos by Steven Paul Whitsitt

Empire Style Revival

High ceilings, lavish drapery, and intricate crown mouldings emulate French First Empire style in this impressive living room. Even the period footstools and tables evoke this popular, early nineteenth century style. Silver and taupe tones affect a formal, majestic air, culminating in a historical look stripped down and simplified for the present day. The splendid mirror above the neoclassic fireplace reveals onlookers and the overhanging balcony.

Design: Diane Durocher, ASID, CID, Diane Durocher Interiors, Inc.
Photography: David Gruol

Lemon-lime colors cool a tropic space. A wet bar offers up beverages for guests as they move between dining and discussion centers.

Design: Lindy Thomas Interiors
Photography: Randall Perry

Perfectly Moulded

Decorative mouldings define and refine this
space, from the coffered ceiling to the col-
umned entryway. The wainscoting and built-in
shelving are particularly useful features.

Design: Debra J. Stein, ASID, Debra J. Interiors
Photography: Randall Perry

Murally Representative

Hand-painted walls and ceiling by Jeannie Garrison mimic the carpet pattern and combine for a formal effect evocative of high Parisian style.

Designed by Charlew Builders
Mural Art by Jeannie Garrison
Photography: Randall Perry

Family
Rooms

A mix of antiques brings a sense of tradition to a kitchen furnished with fresh white kitchen cabinetry. Lofts and lofty accent windows overlook the central family room. A rich red rug anchors the congregational center. An antique leaded glass transom lowers the entryway and embellishes the grand archway between living room and kitchen.

Design: Linda Dickerson Interiors, ASID, IDS
Photos by Steven Paul Whitsitt

Lofty Aspirations

A corner office gets elevated status in this
great open space, outlined in beautiful beams.
A massive stone chimney commands one wall,
while glass blurs the lines between indoors and
out on the gable end.

*Design: Katharine Posillico McGowan, Katharine
Jessica Interior Design, LLC*
Photography: Ivy D Photography, Inc.

Warmly Retro

Shag carpeting and throw pillows recall cool times. An eclectic collection of art and artisan furniture is as entertaining as a diversity gathering of individuals.

Design: Gail Shields Miller, Shields & Company Interiors
Photo by Michael Stratton Photography

Comfort Gallery

Retro textiles furnish a room that doubles as
an art gallery, where works can be contem-
plated at leisure.

Design: Bill Swietek
Photos by Steven Paul Whitsitt

Safari Lounge

Wild and exotic touches make this room a favorite in the owner's weekend home. The visitor is immediately struck by the variety of surfaces included in the walls and ceilings, from rugged exposed ceiling beams, to a stacked stone backing for the wood stove, to the unique plaster and wainscoted walls. Faux tiger skin upholstery graces one of the sofas, and throw pillows embroidered with wild beasts rest in the opposite corners. To one side, a driftwood tree trunk provides natural sculpture, echoed in the unique candleholders on the rough-hewn coffee table. The striking pattern on the area rug adds to the feel of a foreign outpost, as does the rustic ladder leading to a loft.

*Design: Tony Fitzgerald Hawkins, Fitz Interior
    Designs, LLC*
Photography: Maggie Barber

Country Cabin, Redux

A juxtaposition of old and new, conventional and eccentric, the interior of this unique log cabin is decked out in wildly colorful plaid, a whimsical twist on the celebrated pattern of all things alpine and outdoorsy. Exposed log walls and a rugged stone and timber fireplace, how-ever, keep the room firmly rooted in tradition, as a hanging hunting trophy looks out over a massive plaid area rug. A corner armoire lends a touch of polish to this decidedly rustic space.

Design: Bennett Weinstock
Photography: John Armich

Arrayed in shades of burgundy (brown) and gold, this warmly lit reading area is built for comfort. The simple lines of the modern bookcase and coffee table direct attention to the paintings behind the couch, carefully chosen to match the color scheme of the space. Orchids in a sleek glass pot add a touch of natural charm.

Design: Bruce Norman Long
Photography: John Armich

Inspired Opulence

Richly carved woodwork is ubiquitous in this living room, with a massive built-in wrap-around bookcase and desk combination, and a stately wood-accented mantelpiece. Elsewhere, rich colors and patterns adorn the furniture and décor, adding to the sumptuous feel of the room. Leather chairs flank a sofa facing the carved stone fireplace, and a throw pillow that mimics ancient embroidery adds historical charm to the space. Artwork graces all of the walls, whether in the form of oil paintings or delicately painted ceramics.

Design: Eleanore Berman, ASID, Design 2 Interiors
Photography: Russell Abraham

A subdued floral pattern ties this living space together, appearing on throw pillows, footstools, and curtains around the room. Decorative details abound, and the use of potted flowers is prominent. Cozy, long shag carpeting underlies all, and together with velvet upholstery adds warmth and comfort.

Design: Eleanore Berman, ASID, Design 2 Interiors
Photography: Russell Abraham

Classical Accents

Earthy tones give the room an understated, comfortable vibe, enhanced by the matching sets of armchairs and couches. Built-in bookshelves on both sides of the room incorporate cabinets and counter space for attractive custom storage. A bit of antique architectural artwork graces the wall above the couch, depicting a stately building in the neo-classic style that the space emulates.

Design: Evelyn Benatar, ASID, New York Interior Design, Inc.
Photography: Ivy D Photography, Inc.

Getaway Everyday

A mountain retreat theme makes this room
a year-round vacation spot. An unusual antler
collection finds a home in a room handsomely
wainscoted and outfitted with a fall moose
motif. Comfort is key in a friendly gathering
place where friends can chat, or play cards at a
nearby game table.

*Design: Kenneth/Davis Architecture and Interior
   Design*
Photography: Jeffrey Colquhoun

French Court

Fringe and gilded finery adorn this baroque living room. Royal red and gold predominate, softened by pastel greens and blues for a mix that's purely King Louis in appeal, right down to the fleur de lis bookends.

Design: Kenneth/Davis Architecture and Interior Design
Photography: Peter Chin

Wicker rockers are a favorite place for felines to recline, as well as their parents. A deck beyond provides a vicarious view, proffered up from windows placed out at every possible angle.

Design: Neal's Design ~ Remodel
Photography: Frank Kuhlmeier

Holding the Center

Woodwork and brown textiles trace the four squares of this room, adding increments of warming contrast. Built in bookcases by the stone fireplace emphasize the studiousness of the space.

Design: Stephen Pararo, ASID, IIDA, and Leah Bailey, ASID, Pineapple House Interior Design
Photography: Jennifer Lindell

Sunny Symmetry

Blue highlights break up a daisy-bright social spot

Design: Kelley Proxmire, Kelley Interior Designs
Photography: Angie Seckinger

Colorful furnishings provide vantage spots for an incredible stacked stone fireplace rising amidst the structure of a post-and-beam frame.

Design: *Jack McKernon, McKernon Design Associates*
Photography: *Randall Perry*

Fire-side Chat

Den Done Large

Rich wood tones and leather furnishings
add stately, timeless appeal to a great room.
Columns and banisters provide definition for
the space, creating an intimate gathering area
within the spacious surrounds and the glass
wall that opens the view to the outdoors.

Design: Denise Palumbo, Plum and Crimson
*   Interior Design*
Photography: Randall Perry

Lofty Aspirations

This great open space is outlined in beautiful beams. A massive stone chimney commands one wall, while glass blurs the lines between indoors and out on the gable end.

Design: Katharine Posillico McGowan, Katharine Jessica Interior Design, LLC
Photography: Ivy D Photography, Inc.

Women's Retreat

Pinks and greens add cheer to a room furnished with a delightfully eclectic blend of textiles and favorite antiques.

Design: Linda Dickerson Interiors, ASID, IDS
Photos by Steven Paul Whitsitt

111

Blue on Blue

A cobalt couch is a central jewel in this sunny
sitting room where windows connect with a
treetop deck beyond. An ottoman and accent
pillows connect the couch's navy and carpet's
lesser indigo hue with the more earthen tones
that predominate in the room.

Design: Kate Singer Home
Photography: Ivy D Photography, Inc.

A wall mural brings the great outdoors inside for a soft, comforting effect. Wicker furnishings heighten the sense of a wooded retreat, while a favorite heirloom toy and a pleasant repast grace the coffee table.

Design: Joyce Hoshall, ASID, Joyce Hoshall Interiors
Dave Adams Photographer

Bright Delight

This room is all about sunlight, as evidenced
by the wealth of big windows. The owners
installed 2 1/2" horizontal wood blinds to
control the flood of natural light, and provide
privacy after dark. A luxurious sofa, flanked by
end tables and two armchairs, faces a TV set in
a cabinet. In the center, a glass-topped coffee
table is sleek and light, adding to the overall
ambiance of the space.

*Design: Gwen Nagorsky, ASID, of Directions in
Design, Inc.*
Photography: Peter Rymwid

What do people who live in glass houses do? Revel in it! A chaise lounge puts the homeowner in the peak of this glass room, surrounded by exotic furnishings.

Design: Teal Michel Interior Design
Photography: Ben Edmonson

Entertainment
Areas

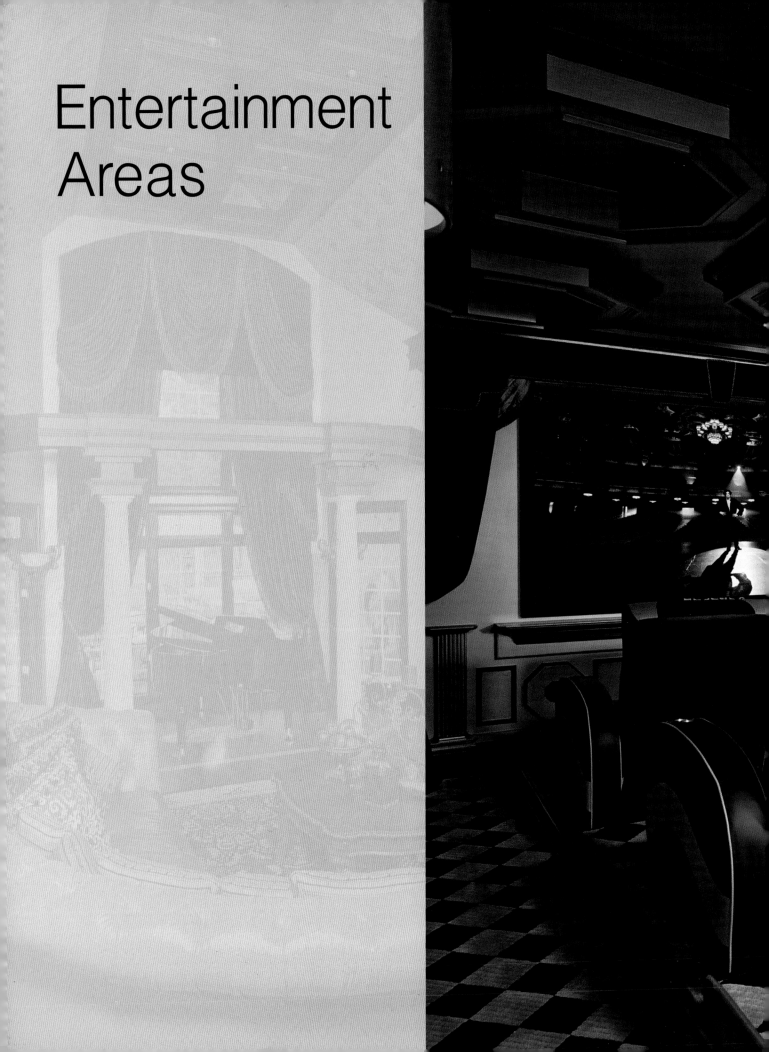

Modern Salon

With an eye toward entertaining, this space
was crafted to create zones where friends can
mix and mingle, accompanied by live entertainment. A support column becomes its own
zone, while a ceiling medallion creates another
congregation area.

*Design: Stephen Pararo, ASID, IIDA, and Nicole
   Bachrach, Pineapple House Interior Design
Photography: Jennifer Lindell*

A passion for piano inspired a dedicated center, with a domed glass light and a parquet floor as fitting accompaniments.

Design: Thomas Cinefro Designs and Spiegel's Decorative Finishes
Photography: Randall Perry

Auspicious Gatherings

A rich tapestry and a Corinthian column create
an aura of historic import in this little nook.
Outfitted with a wet bar, it's a favorite place to
entertain and share spirits with friends.

Design: Joyce Hoshall, ASID, Joyce Hoshall
*   Interiors*
Photography: Dave Adams

Bar None

Burlwood adds an Art Deco veneer to this
exciting home bar, with metallic purple seating
re-emphasizing the *Great Gatsby* good times.

Design: Pamela Crocket Interior Services
Photography: Randall Perry

Rattan furniture and bark cloth upholstery hark back to the happy days of the 1950s. Maple cabinets with a brown glaze top slate tile backsplash and pure black granite countertops. The LED lighting on the inside of the cabinets creates a glow from within.

Design: Skip Shingledecker, CKD, CBD, SA Home Design

Masculine Retreat

This is a gentleman's recreation room in classic style, from the log walls to the richly embellished billiards table.

Design: Phillip Smerling Design
Photography: Randall Perry

Distinctive Diversion

A black and white color scheme unites this sophisticated playroom, down to the billiards table that serves as its main attraction. A zebra skin rug adorns the floor, beside a stylish leather chair and a sculpted table. Under a wide mirror, which serves to enhance the size of the room, rests a spherical sculpture constructed entirely of road signs, adding a touch of color and panache. Lighting in the sloped ceiling casts an ambient glow, and a mod chandelier gives off nightclub vibes.

Design: Bruce Benning Design Associates,
*   Interiors and Lighting*
Photography: Dave Adams

Retro Recreation

Modern and mid-century meet in a too-cool hangout for friends and family, complete with a home bar and modern wine cellar. Low-slung furnishings recreate the way we used to rest, while the rug beneath recalls the bold linoleum patterns of yesterday's ranch home. There are remnants of the old homestead, but in a space that would incorporate the entire house of yesteryear.

Design by Joani Stewart, ASID, IIDA, Montana Avenue Interiors
Photography: Douglas Hill

A lanai – that favorite sheltered room of lucky tropical climate dwellers, opens to a screened pool area. A fire-pit was built into the col-umned supports that define the "room."

Design: Kane Custom Homes
Photography: Randall Perry

Back to Baroque

Exotic leather furnishings outfitted with fringes and finery form the central focus of a great room. A piano sits in the dramatically curtained alcove, while a great flat screen seems almost dwarfed atop a mantel and fireplace surround carved with Gothic sensibility. A nearby wet sink is no less showy, with its finely carved wood details and mottled marble backsplash.

Design: Michelle Chisholm, Interior Dezign by 2 of a Kind
Photography: Steven Paul Whitsitt

Pop Culture

Black and gold create an exciting backdrop for a home theater experience. Prepared for the good times, the homeowners keep snacks at hand. The "lobby" includes a popcorn machine that serves it up hot, just like in the theaters.

Design: Michelle Chisholm, Interior Dezign by 2 of a Kind
Photography: Steven Paul Whitsitt

Delightfully Modern

The striking effect of colorful glass collectibles is reflected both in glass, and in the colorful painting that adorns an ample wall. This spacious, light living room was streamlined with recessed cabinetry, the room artfully divided by a semi-circular couch where colorful pillows create both comfort and style. Picture windows and sliding glass doors blur the lines between this space and the natural surroundings. A modern sculpture supported by a marble pedestal near the windows is another opportunity for the owners to exhibit their sense of style.

Design: Bruce Benning Design Associates,
  Interiors and Lighting
Photography: Dave Adams

A Study in Blue

Opposite Page:
Patterns are essential in this multi-purpose space, as stripes and waves collide on the comfortably upholstered sofas and armchairs. Throughout the room (even on the china displayed in the kitchen nook) the combination of blue and white is front-and-center, providing a theme that ties it all together. On one wall, the contours of the stone are highlighted in white for rustic effect, while bare stone provides a backdrop for an entertainment center encased in simple cabinetry.

Design: Bennett Weinstock
Photography: John Armich

Family gatherings are cozy and bright in a room warmly outfitted against the chill beyond. Shoes warm by the fire, while the family rests on deeply upholstered furniture for electronic entertainment.

Courtesy of the Desert Mountain Community, Scottsdale, Arizona
Design: Hillary Reed Interiors
Photography: Mark Boisclair

Arch Entertainment

Fish tanks flank the grand, double Dutch doorway that opens to reveal the home entertainment center. The triptych built-in is also home
to speakers, for surround sound, all cleverly
disguised as gorgeous woodwork.

*Design: Terri Wesselman, ASID, Omni Design
    Group, Inc.*
Photography: Randall Perry

Sky tones add an ethereal effect to an entertainment room's soft, warm earth colors.

Design: Christina Ribbel Interior Design
Photography: Randall Perry

Libraries
& Dens

Central Workspace

An office area was created using decorative arches and defining columns. The central light adds awe factor, and contemporary blues and animal prints bring the space its edgy, modern appeal.

Design: Joan Waddell Interiors
Photography: Walt Roycroft

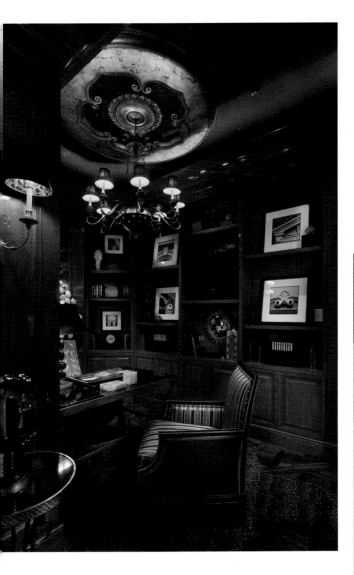

A Love for Literature

This stately neo-classic library houses the owner's sizeable book collection, and provides an inspiring environment for reading and writing. Dentil mouldings abound, even adorning the underside of each bookshelf, and regal mock columns encase the doorway with its lovely transom lights. The spice colored ceiling upholstered in silk taffeta complements the ivory shades of the walls and bookcases for an effect that is at once contemporary and evocative of another time. Finished with a carpet that brings out the darker accents in the walls, this room suggests a wealth of refinement and scholarship.

Design: Bacari Design, Inc.
Photography: Hi Tech Photo

This den has a distinctly masculine essence, with its smoky brown tones and rugged décor. Leather-bound blinds embellish the large bay windows, which house one of a matching set of sofas. Bookcases to the right house a favorite collection, and on the left, a lamp fashioned from an antique tobacco tin creatively lights the space. A giant leather footstool serves as the centerpiece of the den, pictured with a tray for cigars and brandy snifters.

Design: Ellen Baron-Goldstein, Baron-Goldstein Design Associates Ltd.
Photography: Ivy D Photography, Inc.

143

Her Story

A red Venetian plaster finish adds allure to a
feminine library retreat.

Design: Karen E. Keysar Interiors
Photography: Steven Paul Whitsitt

Gorgeous wood paneling on all sides, including the ceiling, make this sitting room a wonder to behold. Finely carved mouldings overhang built-in bookshelves; all stained a dark and beautiful color that complements the lighter leather furniture. Wall-to-wall carpeting is a comfortable touch, and three windows usher in natural light during the day, with Venetian blinds for privacy at night. In compartments over the window transoms, ornamental silver vessels provide refined décor and a dash of polish.

Design: Lori Feldman, FDS, Inc. & Culin &
    Colella, Inc.
Photography: Ivy D Photography, Inc.

Seamstress' Palace

A virtual dream room for any quilter or crafter, this room was dedicated solely to a passion for creation. Open shelves allow fabrics to be stashed in color-coordinated slots, and lots of comfy chairs, and a cutting table, allow the process of creating to follow the sun as it streams through a generous bank of windows. Two favorite pets have their place in the picture, too.

Design: Neal's Design ~ Remodel
Photography: Frank Kuhlmeier

Small
Flats

One World

Instead of trying to hide different rooms in a small, round home, the design opened them up to each other. Here kitchen, sleeping quarters, and living room all communicate through the interior, dismissing some privacy while exploding the sense of space. *Courtesy of the Desert Mountain Community, Scottsdale, Arizona*

Design: Hillary Reed Interiors
Photography: Mark Boisclair

Green Scene

Metal artwork on the wall helped dictate the coppery patina of this room. Retro fabrics add to the sophistication of this green and gold room.

Design: Teal Michel Interior Design
Photography: Mimika Clooney, Charlotte
*   Photobasics*

The soft interplay of grey and beige tones creates a romantic antique haze in this fireside sitting area. It's a muted place to relax, away from the livelier, sun-streamed dining area beyond.

Design by Joani Stewart, ASID, IIDA, Montana
*   Avenue Interiors*
Photography: Greg Crawford

Living Lofty

Cool blues add funky sky appeal to a lofty retreat. A folding screen conceals an exercise machine while letting the light from a bump-out dormer find its way in.

Design: Teal Michel Interior Design
Photography: Ben Edmonson

The Parlor

An octagonal limestone table serves as the centerpiece of this private sitting room, decorated with a mix of authentic antique furniture and a few modern touches. In one corner, a delicately carved cabinet houses a collection of fine porcelain. The sitting area, with beige couches and an oriental privacy screen, is understated and comfortable, and has retractable shutters to control the brightness of the space. In all, the parlor has hints of the art-deco aesthetic, down to the antique mirror on the table holding picture frames and a bowl with flowers.

Design: Bacari Design, Inc.
Photography: Dan Forer

This apartment room successfully combines the clean lines of modern design and the comfortable ambiance of home with abstract artwork hanging from the walls and cozy furniture. The dining room and living room are open to each other, maximizing floor space and enhancing the size of the flat. In the dining area, a Birdseye Maple wood table holds an arrangement of Topiary trees, and is surrounded by curvy upholstered chairs. The living area, with its flat screen TV and sleek glass coffee table, is a gathering place for friends and family, made warmer and more inviting by a calfskin rug, and an expansive curved wall of windows, which illuminate the space.

Design: Eric J. Schmidt Interiors
Photography: Ivy D Photography, Inc.

Silent Picture Show

Plexiglas provides a clear half wall between fireside seating and fine dining in this contemporary setting. Bold use of black and white allows accents, like a delightful lawn bowl, to really impress. Black and White photography brings character, and characters, to the space, as do marble guard dogs by the waterfront windows. The discipline is carried out across two floors, wrapping around into a black and white kitchen area where fresh floral arrangements stand out like firecrackers.

Design: Rona Landman, ASID, Rona Landman Interior Design
Photography: Ivy D Photography, Inc.

Passages

Roman Empire

A gilded passageway offers many opportunities to linger amidst the hand-painted murals, by the central fountain, or in several comfy chairs offered up for comfy seating.

Designed by Charlew Builders; Mural Art by
* Jeannie Garrison*
Photography: Randall Perry

A fire-lit entryway was too wonderful to simply pass by. So petite chairs were found that could cozy up a while, and wine and entertainment were added to the alcove.

Design: Mary Laborde Interior Design
Photos by Steven Paul Whitsitt

Bed & Bath

Crimson Tide

Brilliant scarlet adds joy to this master suite, from the big sleigh-style king bed with its balcony view, to a platform tub that elevates the art of soaking. A chaise lounge big enough for two provides two more reasons to linger in the wash of color of light by day, luxurious isolation by night.

Design: Lori Feldman, FDS, Inc.
Photography: Ivy D Photography, Inc.

Rosy Outlook

Pale peach suffuses a feminine boudoir, outlined in fringes and finery fit for a princess. The room offers a sense of ivory tower, with a four-poster, pedestal view over an isolated, wintry landscape.

Design: Kate Singer Home
Photography: Ivy D Photography, Inc.

Endless Honeymoon

This room is one where the love affair never grows old. The fireplace is ever at the ready to re-ignite a warm glow, and comfortable furnishings make this a great place to be together, both day and night.

Design: Joyce Hoshall, ASID Allied, Joyce Hoshall Interiors
Dave Adams Photographer

White Nights

Fabrics of beiges and off white create the ambiance of this sophisticated bedroom. The dramatic tray ceiling and crystal chandelier highlight all the details in the space.

Design: A.J. Margulis, ASID Allied, Deborah Leamann Interiors
Photography: Tom Grimes

Happy Endings

Unwinding before bed was never so easy! Comfy custom chairs, a big television, and an entirely different dressing room for all the clutter make this a perfect day to put away the cares. A coffered ceiling helps scale down the grand room, creating a false ceiling under a towering roof, the effect doubled by the two tone-walls capped with dark moulding. The sense is of a human scale within the soaring space.

Design: Sara Dickinson, Morgan House Interiors
Photography: Paul S. Bartholomew

Royal Repose

Splendor abounds in a master suite outfitted in comforting finery. Long drapes emphasize the lavish allowance of window and light allotted this space, and soft furnishings allow the owners to luxuriate in it.

Design: Agostino's Design Group
Photography: Randall Perry

Cool grey tones pick up on the sea tones beyond the window, while rich upholsteries create a warm nest from which to enjoy the view.

Design: Kira Krümm Interior Design
Photography: Randall Perry

King's Repose

Rich mouldings and satiny textiles contribute
to the royal atmosphere of this master suite.

Design: Kira Krümm Interior Design
Photography: Randall Perry

Romantic Retreat

Blue toile fabric, on the windows and bed, and upholstered on the walls, present classic garden architecture and contribute to sweet dreams of garden getaways.

Design: Totten McGuirl Fine Interiors
Photography: Paul S. Bartholomew Photography, Inc.

Ladies' Retreat

Shades of blush soften this room, accented with a few dark details. This lofty retreat aspires to regal luxury, and exudes delicate femininity. Lacey patterns adorn the carpet, and sheer, gossamer curtains allow a soft light to flood the room, giving the space an aura of purity and tranquility.

*Design: Maureen Console' ASID Allied, M.
   Console' Interiors*
Photography: Ivy D Photography, Inc.

Pastel Paradise

With multicolored rays emanating from the base of the door jamb, everything about this child's bedroom is bright and colorful, and a fine example of what can be accomplished with a little creativity. The owners used masking tape to help create the wall effects, while the ceiling was sponge-painted to resemble the sky. A carpeted step-up region lends interest to the space, along with a sloping ceiling that traces the roofline.

*Design: Roslyn Schineiderman, ASID, NCIDQ, RS
   Design*
Photography: John Armich

174

This elegant guest bedroom has a subtle floral theme in art prints above the headboard, the curtains, and in vases stocked with fresh flowers atop the tables. Even the wallpaper has an understated flowery pattern. Throughout, dusty rose hues give the space a sense of warm comfort, down to a unique light fixture hanging from the ceiling. The bed itself is ornately carved and has a matching bench at its foot.

Design: Ellen Baron-Goldstein, Baron-Goldstein Design Associates, Ltd.
Photography: Ivy D Photography, Inc.

Gingham Come

Checkerboard browns add country delight to a room staged for sweet dreams. Dentil moulding hugs the crown on two sides of the ceiling, but stays low under a gable eve in order to create a little blue sky.

Design: Kate Singer Home
Photography: Ivy D Photography, Inc.

Memoirs of a Boudoir

A young lady's bedroom gets a geisha style. Tatami mats measure the floor space, while a futon and neatly stacked furnishings trace a low profile around the room's perimeter.

Design by Joani Stewart, ASID, IIDA, Montana Avenue Interiors
Photography: Douglas Hill

Bali Bedroom

Rattan on the walls, a ceiling fan, and a louvered door to the great outdoors contribute to the cabana-like feeling of this "stay-cation" getaway.

Design: Kane Custom Homes
Photography: Randall Perry

Teen Tones

A young girl's room is puffed up in petal-bright colors, with repeating squares to keep it funky.

Design: Diane Paparo Associates
Photography: Immagine 3

177

Guest Station

A guest suite offers a library of books and a
sunlit second home to dear friends and family.

Design: Cheryl A. Van Duyne Interior Design
Photography: Danny Piassick

A star-shaped light cap and wall sconces create atmospheric light ensured to make you look good as you groom yourself before dual sink areas. The semi-gloss of faux grass cloth walls diffuses the light and complements the rich wood tones of the furniture. Custom high gloss mahogany mirrors are an enticing accent, and a pretty facial frame.

Design: Bacari Design, Inc.
Photography: Dan Forer

Bold Bathroom

The hard lines and rectilinear patterns of this modern bathroom lend it a clean and streamlined look, with plenty of glass to provide an airy and light ambiance. The raised washbasin seems to float in the air, and simple faucets complement the tile finish. In the back, a massive shower with stainless steel fixtures is encased with glass, for luxurious bathing amid appealing surroundings. Blonde cabinetry is the subtle power behind this ultra-neat lavatory, providing a wealth of storage space.

Design: Ibarra Rosano Design Architects, Inc.
Photography: Bill Timmerman

Twist on the Twenties

The striking black and white striped walls of this retro bathroom, coupled with the period décor and fixtures, successfully reproduce the essence of 1920s design and aesthetics. A circular mirror typical of the heyday of art deco style hangs above a black granite sink with chic brass handles and faucet. In a corner, coupled with ostentatious potted plants, a flamboyant zebra-striped chair evokes the exuberant excess of the Roaring '20s. Above the lustrous tub, a framed painting nods to jazz culture and produces a splash of vibrant color.

Design: Maureen Console', ASID Allied, M. Console' Interiors
Photography: Ivy D Photography, Inc.

Light Soak

A jetted tub provides a soothing soak with views out in two directions. Side-swept curtains and a sculptured bust enhance fantasies of a Mediterranean getaway, down to the circular light fixtures and the potted plant in the corner. The tub itself is ensconced in marble and dark-stained wood paneling. A plush cushioned stool in subdued salmon helps soften the transition from dreamy water escape to the workaday cares beyond this room.

Design: Pricilla Fried Interior Design/Staging
Photography: Ivy D Photography, Inc.

A guest powder room offers visitors an opportunity to luxuriate alone for a moment in a room rich with earthy textures and hues.

Design: Linda Kleeman, ASID, Kleeman & Associates Interior Design
Photography: Dave Adams

Watery Horizon

A soaking tub offers more than water to soak in. The skyline view beyond is mesmerizing. Should the sun be too intense, however, shade screens lower to cool things off.

Design: Diane Paparo Associates, Ltd.
Photography: Immagine 3

Exalted and Vaulted

A barrel-vaulted ceiling follows the passage of an enormous master suite bath, culminating in the elevated, column flanked pedestal that frames the jetted tub.

Design: Agostino's Design Group
Photography: Randall Perry

Queen's Ablutions

Marie Antoinette would have wanted no less:
a palatial master bath with an elevated stage
for soaking, and a padded vanity pedestal upon
which to perform beauty rituals.

Design: Agostino's Design Group
Photography: Randall Perry

A fireside soak is embellished with decorative, gilded ironwork and carved wooden mouldings on the tub surround. By day the room is soaked in sunshine, by night a chandelier casts a romantic glow in complement to the flickering fire.

Design: Debra J. Stein, ASID, Debra J. Interiors
Photography: Randall Perry

Tub Hub

Tropical hardwoods and rich brown linens define this tiled bath space, where a pedestal tub is the centerpiece.

Design: Kane Custom Homes
Photography: Randall Perry

Onyx stone encases a whirlpool tub beneath the roman arch of a picture window, and adds counter space to vanity areas in an expansive master bath suite.

Design: Diane Boyer Interiors, LLC
Photos by Phillip Ennis

Contributors

Every effort has been made to check and cross check information and to make sure all of our contributors had an opportunity to correct factual errors and fill in missing pieces. Despite a sincere desire to make sure all worthy and creative people get full credit, deadlines come, and some information doesn't. Please send corrections to the author's attention, in writing, so that we can complete or update this list in future printings.

Designers

Agostino's Design Group
Naples, Florida
239-430-9108
www.agostinos.com

Architextures, LLC
Saint Louis, Missouri
314-961-9500
www.architexturesllc.com

Bacari Design Inc.
Washington, D.C.
202-518-0110
www.bacaridesign.com

Baron-Goldstein Design Associates, Ltd.
Roslyn, New York
516-627-8604
www.barongoldsteindesign.com

Bennett Weinstock
Philadelphia, Pennsylvania

Bill Swietek
San Francisco, California
415-933-2170

Bruce Benning Design Associates, Interiors and Lighting
Sacramento, California
916-448-8120
www.benningdesign.com

Bruce Norman Long
New York, New York
212-980-9311
www.bnl-interiordesign.com

Cheryl A. Van Duyne Interior Design
Dallas, Texas
972-387-3070
www.cherylvanduyne.com

Christina Ribbel Interior Design
Naples, Florida
239-261-8903

Clark & Green, Inc.
Great Barrington, Massachusetts
413 528 5180
www.clarkandgreen.com

Culin & Colella, Inc.
Mamaroneck, New York
914-698-7727
www.culincolella.com

Debra J. Interiors
Boynton Beach, Florida
561-243-8000
www.debrajinteriors.com

Deborah Leamann Interiors
Pennington, New Jersey
609-737-3330
www.deborahleamanninterior.com

Design 2 Interiors
San Jose, California
408-284-0100
www.design2interiors.com

Diane Boyer Interiors, LLC
Verona, New Jersey
973-857-5915
www.dianeboyer.com

Diane Durocher Interiors, Inc.
Ramsey, New Jersey
201-825-3832
www.dianedurocherinteriors.com

Diane Paparo Associates, Ltd.
New York, New York
212-308-8390
www.paparo.com

Directions in Design, Inc.
Long Valley, New Jersey
908-852-4228
www.directionsindesigninc.com

Eric J. Schmidt Interiors
New York, New York
212-288-3431
www.ericschmidtinteriors.com

Eva & You Interior Design
Port Jefferson, New York
631-928-7913
www.evaandyou.com

FDS, Incorporated
Greenwich, Connecticut
203-532-2944
www.fdsdesign.com

Fitz Interior Designs, LLC
New York, New York
212-752-6900
www.fitzinteriordesigns.com

Glenn Lawson, Inc.
New York, New York
212-319-3003
www.glennlawson.com

Green Scene Landscape
Canoga Park, California
818-227-0740
www.greenscenelandscape.com

Hillary Reed Interiors
Littleton, Colorado
303-794-0051
www.hridesign.com

Ibarra Rosano Design Architects, Inc.
Tucson, Arizona
520-795-5477
www.ibarrarosano.com

Interior Dezign by 2 of a Kind
Elon, North Carolina
336-684-5287

J.B. Turner & Sons
Oakland, California
510-658-3441
www.jbturnerkitchens.com

Jeannie Garrison
jeanniegarrison.com

Joan Spiro Interiors
Great Neck, New York
516-829-9087

Joan Waddell Interiors
Louisville, Kentucky
502-897-6566

Joyce Hoshall Interiors
Folsom, California
916-756-7538
www.joycehoshall.com

Judith Designs, Ltd.
Greenvale, New York
516-621-1218
www.judithdesignsltd.com

Karen E. Keysar Interiors
La Plata, Maryland
301-753-4069

Kate Singer Home
Huntington, New York
631-261-8376
www.katesingerhome.com

Katharine Jessica Interior Design, LLC
Huntington, New York
631-418-8491
www.kj-id.com

Kelley Interior Designs
Bethesda, Maryland
301-320-2109
www.kelleyinteriordesign.com

Kenneth/Davis Architecture and Interior
 Design
Pompton Plains, New Jersey
973-248-0870
www.kennethdavis.net

Kira Krümm Interior Design
Estero, Florida
239-992-5586
www.kirakrumm.com

Kleeman & Associates Interior Design
Sacramento, California
916-489-3800
www.LindaKleeman.com

Leku Eder
Danville, California
925-820-8012
www.lekueder.eastbaysocial.com

Linda Dickerson Interiors
Durham, North Carolina
919- 403-1433
www.lindadickerson.citysearch.com

Lindy Thomas Interiors
Naples, Florida
239-254-8822
www.lindythomasinteriors.com

LMK Interiors
Lafayette, California
925 962-9610
www.lmkinteriors.com

Mary Laborde Interior Design
St. Simons Island, Georgia
912 634-2224

McKernon Design Associates
Brandon, Vermont
888.484.4200
www.mckernongroup.com

M. Console' Interiors
Northport, New York
631-757-0002

Metropolitan Cabinet & Countertop
Norwood, Massachusetts
800-698-8999
www.metcabinet.com

Montana Avenue Interiors
Santa Monica, California
310-581-1960
www.montanaaveinteriors.com

Morgan House Interiors
Clinton, New Jersey
908-735-6654
www.morganhouseinteriors.com

New York Interior Design, Inc.
Great Neck, New York
516-482-4787
www.nyinteriordesign.com

Omni Design Group, Inc.
Oakton, Virginia
703-652-3141

Pamela Crockett Interior Services
Naples, Florida
239 821 6243

Peter Budeiri + Associates, Architects
New York, New York
212-683-2008
www.budeiriarchitects.com

Phillip Smerling Design
Great Barrington, Massachusetts

Pineapple House Interior Design
Atlanta, Georgia
404-897-5551
www.pineapplehouse.com

Plum and Crimson Interior Design
Clifton Park, New York
518-373-2009
www.plumandcrimson.com

Pricilla Fried Interior Design/Staging
Bronx, New York
917-533-8074

Richlin Interiors
Naples, Florida
239-659-3007
www.richlininteriors.com

Rona Landman Interior Design
New York, New York
212-996-8171
www.ronalandmaninteriordesign.com

RS Design
Willow Grove, Pennsylvania
215-659-4879
www.rozasid.com

SA Home Design
San Antonio, Texas
210-520-3100

Shields & Company Interiors
New York, New York
212-679-9140
www.shieldsinteriors.com

Spiegel's Decorative Finishes
Naples, Florida
239-273-1100
www.spiegelsdecorativefinishes.com

Teal Michel Interior Design
Charlotte, North Carolina
704-554-7035
www.tealmichelasid.com

Thomas Cinefro Designs
Naples, Florida
239-784-3958
thomascinefro@aol.com

Totten McGuirl Fine Interiors
Basking Ridge, New Jersey
908-580-9572
www.totten-mcguirl.com

Victor Liberatore Interior Design
Stevenson, Maryland
410-486-6942
www.victorliberatoreinteriordesign.com

Other Contributors

Amedore Homes
Albany, New York
518-456-1010
www.amedorehomes.com

Ambiance Unlimited
Albany, New York
518-373-0770
www.ambiancesystems.com

Charlew Builders, Incorporated
Schenectady, New York
518-355-7083
www.charlew.com

Belmonte Builders
Clifton Park, New York
518-371-1000
www.belmontebuilders.com

Desert Mountain Community
Scottsdale, Arizona
www.desertmountain.com

Kane Custom Homes
Naples, Florida
239-394-6368

Neal's Design ~ Remodel
Cincinnati, Ohio
513-489-7700
www.neals.com

Metro Asset Management Inc.
Chicago, Illinois
312 493-7588

Photographers

Russell Abraham
www.rabrahamphoto.com

Dave Adams
www.daveadamsphotography.com

Photography by John Armich
www.johnarmich.com

Maggie Barber
www.magdalenebarber.com

Paul S. Bartholomew Photography, Inc.
www.psbphoto.com

Mark Boisclair Photography
www.markboisclair.com

Peter Chin
www.peterchin.net

Mimika Clooney, Charlotte Photobasics
Charlotte, North Carolina

Jeffrey Colquhoun
Camden, Maine

Fred Donham of Photographer link
www.photographerlink.com

Ivy D Photography
www.ivydphotography.com

Ben Edmonson Photographer
www.blackdogimages.com

Phillip Ennis Photography
www.phillip-ennis.com

Dan Forer
www.forer.com

Alan Gilbert
www.photopian.com

Jeff Green Photography
www.jgreenphoto.com

Tom Grimes
www.tomgrimes.com

David Gruol
www.davidgruolphotography.com

Douglas Hill
www.doughill.com

Hi Tech Photo
www.hi-techphoto.com

Immagine 3
imm3@iol.it

Jennifer Krogh
Brooklyn, New York
917-685-6925

Jennifer Lindell
912-294-0172

Scott Moore
www.scottmoorephoto.com

Randall Perry Photography
www.randallperry.com

Danny Piassick Photography
www.piassick.com

Ben Ritter Photography
ben@benritter.com

Walt Roycroft Photography
www.wrphotography.com

Peter Rymwid
www.peterrymwid.com

Angie Seckinger
www.angieseckinger.com

Michael Stratton Photography
mkstratton@nyc.rr.com

Bill Timmerman
www.billtimmerman.com

Steven Paul Whitsitt Photography
whitsittphoto@yahoo.com